To Our Readers:

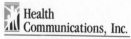

Cindy — Wishing you

ORGANIZED SERENITY

A Practical Guide For Getting It Together

Jann Mitchell

Jann Mitchell

Health Communications, Inc.
Deerfield Beach, Florida

©1992 Jann Mitchell

ISBN 1-55874-148-8

Publisher: Health Communications, Inc.
3201 S.W. 15th Street
Deerfield Beach, Florida
33442-8190

Dedication

For . . .

My husband, TED, whose recovery guided me toward my own.

My friend, TAMERA, whose organization led me from chaos.

My mother, JANICE, whose responsibility set an example.

My father, BLAKE, whose admonition "sloppy room, sloppy mind" proved to be correct.

Contents

Introduction V

1. The Courage To Change 1

2. Who Am I? 11

3. Managing Your Time 25

4. Organizing Concepts 39

5. Notebooks And Lists 53

6. You 65

7. Reconnecting 85

Bibliography 99

Introduction

Chaos is not conducive to serenity.

This is a book for all recovering people who instinctively sense this truth but aren't sure how to achieve it. No matter the addiction — alcohol, drugs, food, people, gambling, sex — the goal of recovery is the same: abstinence and a peaceful, productive and satisfying life.

People in my family are recovering from chemical dependency and eating disorders, while I work daily at recovering from relationship addiction and the general compulsiveness of my co-dependence. Some days I'm more successful than others. I'm also recovering from pure slobbery.

It began as a teenager. With my first taste of procrastination, I was hooked. I waited until the night before a paper was due to begin work. I crammed for tests at the last minute. What I wanted to wear was never clean, ironed or possessed all its buttons.

As a young bride, my slobbery accelerated. I was so disorganized, my new husband had to eat breakfast on the coffee table because last night's dinner dishes littered the kitchen table. I dodged people I'd never thanked for wedding, birthday or Christmas gifts. My children outgrew clothes before I mended or ironed them. The baby's pacifier finally turned up after she was in school. Bills surfaced months after they were due. Dinner was often a draw because I'd forgotten to thaw.

Divorce brought even more responsibility — and removed someone to blame.

As a newspaper reporter I had deadlines to meet but I'd put off setting up an interview until the last minute. Notes were lost in the heaps of papers on my desk. Phone numbers scribbled on scraps of paper disappeared. The receipt I needed was always in another purse. I usually gave myself 15 minutes to get anywhere: across the street or across town. Invariably I was late. By the time I was finally ready to go on a business trip or vacation, I was too pooped to work or relax. I signed up for night classes but dropped out. Sometimes the car ran out of gas or had to be towed because I put off regular service.

Throughout this mess I was enmeshed in a long affair with a married alcoholic. Then a series of compulsive relationships with other problem-plagued people allowed me to feel superior.

At home and at work, in my head and in my heart, life was chaotic, disorganized, topsy-turvy and unmanageable.

Then I fell in love with an alcoholic (unmarried) for whom I helped stage an intervention — not realizing then that a Higher Power was working toward getting us both well. He got sober, we were married and a few years later we divorced as I began the painful process of my own recovery. He began looking at some of his deeper issues and we found each other again.

During all this a friend who had developed into an organizational expert passed her helpful hints on to me. Gradually, painfully I progressed from slob toward serene, combining the principles of recovery with the principles of organization and time management.

No matter what we are recovering from, we know that successful recovery is more than simply (or not so simply) not drinking, overeating or using. Successful recovery also means growth and a sense of peace — serenity — which comes from being responsible and trying to do what's right.

From the time we were small we have been nagged, preached at and scolded about what's right, especially in the areas of organization and time management.

"No TV until your room is clean." "Any job worth doing is worth doing well." "Get up now or you'll be late." "Don't do a half-way job." "Sloppy room, sloppy mind." "Learn how to organize your time or you'll never graduate . . . get into college . . . get a job . . . hold a job." "Get your act together!"

We may have seen some merit in their arguments, but many of us rebelled against the attempt to control us. Or we may have become tidy little robots in attempts to gain parental approval. Either way, we lost touch with our own sense of what was right for us, our own comfort level regarding how we organized our surroundings and managed our time. Our addictions added to the chaos.

As recovering people we are beginning — finally — to listen to our inner voices. We try to be honest. To recognize our feelings and voice them. To make amends to others by doing the right thing today. We discover that these principles carry over into every aspect of our lives — except for getting organized.

But it can happen! We've already done the really tough work by admitting we had a disease and committing ourselves to recovery. Already we feel better — and have more time and perhaps more money.

This book is intended to help us feel even better about ourselves as we learn to eliminate the clutter and the chaos from our lives. By getting organized, our surroundings will reflect the person we're becoming — calm, uncomplicated, responsible, serene. And we'll have even more time to do the things we've always wanted to do.

If *you* want to . . .

- Grow less harried
- Become more efficient
- Feel more relaxed
- Suffer less guilt
- Make time for fun
- Find what you want when you want it.

Then find a clean place to sit down and keep reading.

And welcome to the wonderful fellowship of recovering slobs!

ONE

The Courage To Change

*It's like I just woke up —
now I have to get out of bed.*

— AA member, two months sober

· · · ·

The sunshine is as bright as Don's new attitude as he pulls away from the treatment center and onto the freeway. He's one month into a new way of thinking, a new way of living. Don is a little afraid, starting this clean and sober new life without the familiar structure of family but he's hopeful too.

He pulls into the driveway of his condo, tugs open the garage door — and groans. No room. He parks the car near the front door and walks into the stench of a month-old mess. A new way of thinking, sure — but how will he ever get his surroundings in order?

Sally kisses the kids goodbye, shoving dollars into each small hand so they can buy lunch at school. She'd planned to stop at the grocery store on the way home from her support group last night, but she'd got to talking and there just wasn't time.

There had always been time to binge, but never for much else. At last she was finding a way out of this compulsion, she thought, making her usual dash for the bus. But what about the rest of her disorderly life?

As Jill grabs up her duffle bag to leave with Bob for the weekend workshop on co-dependency, she casts a baleful glance around her office. She's apprehensive about the pain this weekend may bring, but she's glad to escape the mess on her desk — the piles of papers she's procrastinated sorting, the files she can't decide where to put.

Jill is having more and more insights into how her childhood affects her behavior today, but all that hard work leaves her with minimum energy for the day-to-day aspects of organization. She's beginning to change the way she does things, but she despairs of ever getting on top of the paperwork at work and at home.

Notes To Myself

Don, Sally, Jill and Bob are recovering people eager to practice their newly acquired skills and to continue growing as the loving, responsible people they were before addiction ensnared them. They have new tools, supportive new friends and reams of reading and meditation materials.

What they don't have is the foggiest notion of how to apply their new knowledge to the everyday untidiness of their lives — the backlog of papers on their desks, the mishmash of bills atop the dresser, the heap of treasures and trash in the basement, the miasma of activities they're committed to but don't really care about.

The Same Principles Apply

Sure *First Things First* seems like it could apply to the more mundane activities of home and work, but how do you get started when you don't know what comes first: paying the overdue bills after finding where the heck they are, watering the dying plants, catching up with correspondence at work or stocking the refrigerator so you can make dinner when the table is cleared of a half-finished puzzle?

The principles used in the best addiction treatment programs and self-help and 12-Step recovery programs can be applied to the dizzying details at home and on the job.

We'll examine the areas of our lives we want to change. We'll determine how to make those changes simply and we'll learn how to maintain our new system of organization by continually putting First Things First.

Note that "serenity" comes first in the Serenity Prayer: "God, grant me the *Serenity* to accept the things I cannot change, the *Courage* to change the things I can, and the *Wisdom* to know the difference."

Most of you will agree that serenity is paramount to successful recovery. Yet who can remain serene when there are no clean clothes, your desk is overflowing with mail and phone messages, your car's so full of junk it's

Notes To Myself

too embarrassing to carpool — and you haven't the foggiest idea where to start straightening out the tangles of home or work?

The key is in knowing what we can control and what we can't. As recovering people, we have acknowledged there are aspects of our lives we can't control. But we can control our time, our physical surroundings, our feeling of accomplishment and our sense of living our lives as we choose.

We also know where the compulsive quest for perfection has led in the past — straight into the arms of addiction. What we're after here is an organized setting in which to practice our new skills of recovery and enjoy its rewards.

We are not slow learners so much as we are slow unlearners. By recovering, we have chosen to cast off — like old skins which no longer fit — ideas and behaviors we have outgrown.

In his best-selling book, *The Road Less Traveled*, Dr. M. Scott Peck suggests that humankind's "original sin" is laziness. He contends each of us has a core of laziness that staves off spiritual growth as we avoid doing what is inevitably good for us. Disorganization — unreturned phone calls, unmade beds, late bills — is no sin, but perhaps ignoring the inner nudge to change is.

In other words, feeling "fed up with this mess" may be our Higher Power's way of telling us to clean up our act.

12 Good Reasons To Get Organized ____

Let's take that magic number 12 that is steering so many of us toward serenity and look at a dozen good reasons for getting organized:

1. It fosters responsibility.
2. It reduces frustration.
3. It provides a feeling of accomplishment.
4. It helps us put First Things First.
5. It can assist us in making amends.
6. It forms new habits to replace the old destructive ones.
7. It frees us to enjoy our wonderful new lives.

Notes To Myself

8. Sloppy surroundings reflect sloppy thinking, which can lead to slip- pery thinking.
9. It makes constructive use of our new-found time.
10. It puts the chaos of unmanageabil- ity further behind us.
11. Our orderly surroundings will properly reflect the new us.
12. We deserve serene surroundings.

You can probably add a few more reasons of your own, depending on your circumstances. Organization isn't regarded as a job to tackle in addition to recovery, but as a means of supple- menting and reinforcing recovery.

The purpose of getting organized is to have more time for the joys of living — more satisfaction and some guilt-free fun. Our goal isn't to have the tidiest desk in the office or the cleanest home on the block. It's not to become an efficiency expert, compul- sively clocking each movement, timing each task. We simply want to become organized enough at home and at work so that life's relentless minutiae

don't hinder our primary goal: successful recovery.

Our first step toward organized serenity must be knowing what we
want. To do that, we must know who
we are and what's important to us.

Only then — after we've defined
our values — can we set goals, estab-
lish priorities and get to work at free-
ing our lives of the sinister C's: Chaos,
Clutter and Confusion.

Before peeking inside ourselves,
let's make a quick outside appraisal.

Things I Want To Change _____

In what areas would you like to be
more organized and feel more in control? Check those you'd like to change
or fill in your own in the spaces provided.

____ Bill-paying
____ Car maintenance
____ Child care
____ Closet organization
____ Correspondence
____ Daily planning
____ Desk organization

Notes To Myself

___ Dinner hour
___ Entertaining
___ Family activities
___ Fitness
___ Free time
___ Hobbies
___ Meal preparation
___ Morning rush
___ Paper-handling
___ Photo albums
___ Project completion
___ Reading
___ Recovery
___ Remembering birthdays, etc.
___ School work
___ Service work
___ Shopping
___ Social life
___ Holidays
___ Housekeeping
___ Kitchen organization
___ Laundry
___ List-making
___ Love life
___ Lunch breaks
___ Spiritual growth
___ Storage
___ Transition time

____ Vacations
____ Wardrobe
____ Work habits

____ _____
____ _____

Decidedly there are some things
you'd like to change? Let's keep in
mind . . .

A Recovering Slob's Prayer

*"God, grant me the SERENITY of an
organized life with leisure time, the COUR-
AGE to change my habits to ensure these
joys and the WISDOM to be flexible."*

TWO

Who Am I?

You don't need to be a new you,
but the real you.

— Arthur Hammons, Unity Minister

. . . .

What's the first thing that comes to mind when someone asks, "Who are you?"

Is your reply wife, son, parent — or alcoholic, bulimic, compulsive gambler? Or do you think occupation — salesperson, homemaker, student, doctor, trucker, artist?

Let's go beyond our roles, addictions, occupations — to the person deep inside, the "real you" who was there when you were just 10 years old, 15, 25, 40 — the essential you who has always longed for . . . what?

Before we can set goals, determine values and priorities, we have to know what's important to us — who we are and what we want. For many of us, it's been so long since we were clear-thinking enough to examine our wants and needs that now in sobriety and abstinence we're not even sure.

11

But there are simple ways to get back in touch with that dreaming child, that yearning adolescent, that aspiring young adult who's hidden within each of us.

However what if addiction began so early we never even reached those stages? What if we've never known who we are and what we want?

It's possible to find out. The process doesn't have to involve extensive therapy or even intensely deep introspection.

Instead of roles, let's look at wishes, fantasies and daydreams. Call it an inventory of the heart. Our answers indicate what is important to us. Our longings are our Higher Power echoing from deep within, directing us, guiding us. We may not be sure who we are in our heads, but our hearts will give us hints if we'll "be still and know."

Finish The Sentence

Without thinking and analyzing, just feeling, complete these sentences:

Notes To Myself

Notes To Myself

I've always wanted to . . .
(run my own business, move to Alaska, play piano)

I wish I was more . . .
(outgoing, studious, humorous, healthy)

You're getting the idea. Finish these on your own:

I'd really like to _____

_____

I'd like people to see me as _____

_____

When I'm gone, I hope people remember me for _____

_____

It's depressing to _____

Why don't I have _____

If I had just six months to live, I'd ____

_____

_____

My idea of a perfect day is _____

_____

_____

I want to be _____

It's really important to me to _____

_____

I've never really enjoyed _____

_____

I'd like to try _____

I would _____

If I wasn't so _____

Do you see some daydreams, some of the undiluted you coming through? Let's go on.

Set Up A Self Shelf _____

Clear one bookshelf at home or work. This is your "self shelf" on which will go only material that interests you.

Keep books, magazines, newspaper clippings, brochures, travel folders, classified ads, job descriptions, school folders, hobby information, music, recovery pamphlets or inspirational literature.

As the shelf fills up, you will develop a picture of what you're about — not only giving you a sense of self and something to fill in those blanks on questionnaires about "personal interests," but it could start you on a new hobby, an avocation or even a new career. Your shelf could lead you to a church or a vacation spot, to plays, lectures or interest groups you had no idea existed.

Go ahead, be "shelfish!"

Make Three Wishes

Wishing is the first step toward having. Make three wishes each in these areas of your life:

Recovery

I wish _____

I wish _____

I wish _____

Personal

I wish _____

I wish _____

I wish _____

Career

I wish _____

I wish _____

I wish _____

Family

I wish _____

I wish _____

I wish _____

Analyze Your Dreams _____

Psychologists say that our dreams are messages from our subconscious, that we can learn eight times faster what's really going on by studying our dreams than by hashing it over intellectually.

Scientists who specialize in sleep studies say every human being dreams at least two hours per night. If deprived of dream time (by being awakened as they begin to dream), humans will hallucinate. People who say "I never dream" simply can't remember their dreams.

You can begin remembering your dreams by realizing they can be important, and by telling yourself the night before that you *will* remember. Upon awakening, jot your dreams

Notes To Myself

down, noting the plot, the "characters" and how you felt. I keep a separate dream journal. It has helped immeasurably in recovering from relationship addiction. Writing down and analyzing my dreams helps me see how I really feel deep down without the chorus of "shoulds" and "what ifs" that interfere during waking hours.

Read books about dream interpretation but beware those that glibly equate water with sex, a house with security, etc. Everyone has their own dream language or symbolism. With practice you'll decipher your own dream code.

Try Something New

Once a week try something you've never done.

Go to a square dance, a boxing match, a foreign movie or an ethnic restaurant. Pick up a book or magazine on a subject you know nothing about. Drive through a different part of town. Strike up a conversation with a stranger. Watch a TV show you've never seen, listen to a different radio station. Talk to someone you don't really know at work or school. Attend a religious service, another recovery group, a public lecture, a concert.

What did you enjoy? The real you is taking shape with each new discovery. Try it again!

Fantasize

Let your imagination run wild and fill in the blanks again:

If I had just a year to live, I'd *(have more fun, change jobs, spend more time with family)*

If money were no problem, I would ___

_____

Just once before I die, I would like to

_____

It would be wonderful if the family could _____

_____

A trip-of-a-lifetime would be _____

_____

Notes To Myself

What running theme about yourself do you see emerging? Are you a homebody or an adventurer? Do you see yourself soloing or spending most of your time with others? How close is your present life to what's emerging in this chapter?

Determining Your Values _____

Now that you're developing a sense of self, you're ready to determine some values. Consider the following values and feel free to add some of your own:

Recovery
Family
Spouse/lover
Health/fitness
Finances
Security
Travel
Friendships
Career
Home
Hobbies/recreation
Spirituality
Education

Success

_____

_____

_____

_____

Which are most important to you?
List five:

1. _____

2. _____

3. _____

4. _____

5. _____

Now we can move on to goals, and
the activities necessary to achieve
them.

For instance, let's take recovery as
a major value — that's something we
all have in common. Let's follow the
suggestion of time management specialist Diana Silcox and set up a sheet
that looks something like this:

VALUE: My continuing recovery.

GOAL: To remain abstinent, increase my serenity.

Notes To Myself

ACTIVITIES:

1. Attend support group meetings regularly.
2. Read related literature daily.
3. Meditate at least once each day.
4. Make new friends who are recovering themselves or who do not share my addiction.
5. Get a sponsor.
6. Become a sponsor.
7. Volunteer to chair a meeting, make coffee, clean up.
8. Volunteer for service work.
9. Share my experience with others who are suffering.
10. Educate myself by reading everything I can about my addiction.

When we understand our values (what is important to us) and our goals in living out our values, it becomes easier to decide what to do and what not to do. For instance, I am often asked to speak. Years ago, flattered to be asked and eager for an audience, I would say yes to anyone. Since determining what's important to me and setting my goals (encouraging young writers and people working on recovery from co-dependence), I say yes only to speaking on those two topics. Other requests are easily answered with a "No, thanks" — without explanations, rationalizations or feeling guilty about saying no.

Let's look at another value — *friendship:*

VALUE: Friendships.

GOAL: Make new friends, keep valued old friends.

ACTIVITIES:

1. Socialize after support group meetings.
2. Open up to others.
3. Risk — invite people to coffee who I'd like to know better.
4. Have lunch with someone new each week.
5. Invite friends to a potluck, asking each to bring food and a friend.
6. Write more letters.
7. Call someone I haven't seen for a while.

Notes To Myself

Notes To Myself

8. Demonstrate my interest in others by smiling, being interested.
9. Do a favor for someone.
10. Meet the parents of my children's friends.

Don't goals seem easier to accomplish with a list of steps leading toward them? No goal is impossible. Just look at yourself — all those months, years of suffering. Did you ever dream you could experience the joys of recovery? Never say never.

Don't be intimidated that you can't reach a goal because you have no formal training. You've been planning and reaching goals all of your life — just look at how hard you planned and schemed to practice your addiction without interference. We're all master planners. Now we can use that proven ability constructively.

Values change as our lives change. Evaluate yours periodically. Redefining values will mean changing goals. That's up to you.

Remember, don't set too many goals at one time. *Easy Does It!*

THREE

Managing Your Time

The trouble with doing nothing is you never know when you're done.

— AA member

• • • •

"If I could put time in a bottle . . ." sang the late Jim Croce. Many of us did and only now in recovery are we discovering that the world keeps right on ticking.

At first we may wonder just how we'll fill up all this newly discovered time, now that we're not spending all evening in a bar or with our noses in a refrigerator (or someone's else's business). As our interests and activities expand, we grow increasingly aware that time is a precious commodity, that we can't possibly pack all we want to accomplish and experience into 24 hours.

This is why time management is important, especially to those of us who may feel we need to make up for lost time. We can't do it all, but we can make time for the activities we find valuable. First, we must set priorities.

Setting Priorities _____

We can't make up for years of neglect by doing everything in a day or a week. We can only put *First Things First* and tackle the projects which seem the most crucial. That's known as setting priorities.

We can designate our priorities with an A-B-C, 1-2-3, high-medium-low rating system, but the ever-present question remains time management expert Alan Lakein's, *"What's the best use of my time right now?"* When we're stymied about what to do next, when we find ourselves procrastinating, when we feel pressured, asking and answering that question can put us back on track.

If your workday has been a bear — and recovery is a priority — this would mean going to a meeting this evening instead of bowling with a friend. Setting priorities and making lists doesn't mean rigidity or foregoing pleasure. It simply helps us put First Things First.

Notes To Myself

If you have numerous things you'd like to work on this week, try making four headings: *Musts, Try, Start* and *Optional.* Do the Musts first, tackle some Starts, attempt a Try if you have time and go for the Optionals only if everything else is completed.

For example, the car is 1,000 miles overdue for an oil change, two bills must be paid by the end of the week, you owe your grandmother a letter, a work project is due at the end of the month, you should start thinking about a birthday gift for Kathy, the dog needs a bath and you need a topic for chairing next week's support group meeting.

We'll look at list-making in a later chapter, but your weekly To Do list might look like this:

Must — car bills.

Start — work projects, letter, think of meeting topic.

Try — bathing dog.

Optional — shopping for birthday gift.

If you didn't get to the dog or gift, put it on next week's Must list.

Scheduling _____

Many of us believe that if God has a plan for our lives, the least we can do is have a plan for the day. We do this by deciding, *One Day At A Time*, what the most important tasks or activities are.

After we know what we want to get done, we must make the time. Notice that's *make time*, not find time. True, tasks must be fitted in among our duties, but the difference between making and finding time is that we set a specific time aside, rather than just hoping it will turn up. We work it in. We don't merely wish for it.

There are various ways to do this. Organization specialist Tamera Smith Allred defines five basic, daily time management plans:

1. Time Slot
You block tasks by the clock. For example, up at 7 a.m., at work by 8:30, make *To Do* list at 9, make phone calls at 9:15, etc. This system is good for people who have trouble getting started. The clock becomes a prompter.

2. Deadline

Have report finished by 11 a.m., laundry done by noon, new stock shelved by 3 p.m., etc. This system is effective for people who seem to need something hanging over their heads — and it promises periods of freedom to the competitive sorts who enjoy playing beat-the-clock.

3. Day-To-Day

The night before or each morning, list what needs to be done and plan to tackle each item accordingly (perhaps incorporating one of the above methods). This works well for people whose workdays vary greatly and is truly a *One-Step-At-A-Time* system.

4. Ladder

This is a loosely-ordered plan in which you simply note general tasks to be accomplished, such as, tidy house or office, work on project, creative time, correspondence, time alone. This plan gives the basically self-disciplined a lot of leeway yet some sense of structure.

5. *Alternating Plan*

This may incorporate different methods for people with varying schedules — it is handy if you work part-time, divide your time between field and office, are responsible for children some days or you or a spouse work swing shifts.

Adopting a plan is fundamental to organization, but the plan must fit your needs if it is to work. Examine your daily activities, consider the variety of responsibilities involved and perhaps keep a log of several days to see how your day stacks up. Then adopt a plan, modify it to suit your needs and stick with it.

A truly *Keep-It-Simple* approach involves making a weekly list of tasks, then working them into a daily list.

Looking at the week's list noted above, let's set aside a half-hour Sunday evening to develop a topic for the meeting. Monday morning we can make an outline of what we need to do for the work project. We can pay

Notes To Myself

the bills Monday evening after dinner and since we already have pen in hand, let's also polish off that letter to Grandma. We can leave for work a half hour earlier Tuesday morning and swing by the quick-change oil place or plan on changing the oil ourselves first thing Saturday morning. Let's see if our spouse will wash the dog while we're busy with that. Lunch hours are already taken up: Monday (Al-Anon) and Tuesday (Adult Children of Alcoholics), so Wednesday noon let's browse in a couple of stores for Kathy's gift.

Jot each of these tasks and time onto the daily To Do list. Bingo! All those things we've meant to do are as good as done.

Flexibility

As we master scheduling and lists, we must guard against our basic compulsiveness in favor of flexibility. Schedules are meant to guide us, not rule us.

After all, what's more important, paying the bills immediately after dinner as planned for Monday or responding to the person from your support group who just phoned and really needs to talk? So what if we were just leaving to catch a 7 o'clock movie when good friends drop in . . . can't we catch it tomorrow night?

As we follow the motto *First Things First*, let's remember it refers to what is truly important, not merely what we have placed first on a list. As the poster says, "Life is what happens while you're making other plans."

Time Savers

It's been said that time is money. Would we scatter dollar bills to the winds? Yet we do just that by frittering away time on tasks that don't require perfection, on activities we don't really enjoy, on chores we truly hate.

How can we save these dimes of time that so easily add up to dollar days? By . . .

Delegating Responsibility

We don't hesitate to hire experts (doctors, lawyers, repair people) for

Notes To Myself

Notes To Myself

some things, so why are we reluctant to have other people take over so many of our other personal tasks? Believing we alone can handle them sets us up to be controllers (and martyrs) and deprives others of assuming responsibility. When delegating, we can specify what needs to be done (even write it out) but then we must get out of the way and let the other person handle it their way. Just as we're learning to Let Go And Let God, so must we learn to let go and let someone else.

Delegating helps free us from the compulsive self-reliance that goes hand in hand with co-dependence. Delegating can help us avoid becoming what Patricia O'Gorman and Philip Oliver-Diaz call "prisoners of our own competence."

Buying Time

Are there things you'd rather do than wash the car, clean house, run errands? Just because you know how to do something doesn't mean you

have to spend precious time on it —
not when other people are willing to
supply that service for a price. You
don't feel guilty paying someone to
cook for you when you eat at a restaurant so why assume you have to
type your own papers or paint your
own fence? Did you worry about the
money that went for drugs, booze,
gambling or binge food? Buying a service from others is buying time and
freedom for yourself.

Bartering

If money is tight, consider trading
one service for another. Can you fix
a car in exchange for having your
house painted? Can you trade a weekend's childcare for a child-free
weekend yourself? Would you take a
co-worker's shift in trade for a week's
free ride to work? Your recovery
group no doubt draws people with
varied skills. Keep your ears open to
possibilities.

Notes To Myself

Speaking Up

To get help, ask for it from family members, support group members, co-workers, friends. Say no when asked to take on yet another responsibility or an activity you don't enjoy. You needn't make elaborate explanations. (Remember that "no" is a complete sentence.) Avoid interruptions of your time by stating that you must be left alone. Let others know when you are free. Tell bosses and teachers when you're feeling overloaded. If you don't take care of yourself, who will?

Time Makers

We can actually make useful time out of dead time in several ways.

Work While Waiting

Turn snatches of time spent waiting into time spent working, relaxing or recovering. While waiting to see the doctor or meet a client for lunch, write a letter or make notes for a project, read a paperback or clipped article, meditate or review recovery literature. Stuck in a traffic jam? Dictate correspondence or ideas, play soothing music, take a personal inventory. While awaiting telephone call-backs, open mail or begin a task, take a coffee break or daydream, repeat the Serenity Prayer or count your blessings.

Do Double-Duty

Read resource material or review recovery literature while you eat lunch. Fold laundry or polish shoes while you watch television. Scrub the tub when you bathe and set the table when you put away dishes. Do homework reading or plan a party while riding the bus. Walk briskly or jog while walking the dog.

Group Chores

Make and return all phone calls at once. Save errands for a specific time like Saturday mornings. Pay bills and catch up on correspondence while you're seated with paper and pen. Water the yard or wash the dog while you're washing the car. Make the bed before or after dressing.

Go For Results

When time's at a premium and you're not sure what to do, take action that will produce the most significant or effective results. Write a job query, not a thank-you note. Straighten the livingroom, not a closet. Make a sales call, not a bank deposit. Get up earlier, don't sleep in.

Time To Be

Let us realize, though, that time is not for saving — it's for savoring. Everyday, several times a day, do nothing. Sit and breathe. Listen to birds chirping. Watch a bug crawl. Feel how good it is simply to be alive.

Let's guard against being what John Bradshaw calls "human doings instead of human beings." This is the addiction of workaholism, feeling we need to be constantly accomplishing to justify our existence, feel good about ourselves or have the approval of others.

When we are truly free, we can simply be.

<u>**Notes To Myself**</u>

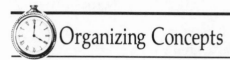

FOUR

Organizing Concepts

Chaos is optional.

— The Author

• • • •

Dr. Bob Smith, co-founder of Alcoholics Anonymous, summarized the AA's 12 Steps as "Trust God, clean house and help others."

That cleaning house refers, of course, to Steps 4 to 11 in which we clean up our act. Let's extend that reference — take it literally — to clear our physical surroundings of chaos.

Let's do it with the three P's of Organized Serenity:

- *Picture* what you want — how you want your surroundings to look and feel, how you want your life to be.
- *Plan* how to get it — establishing values, setting goals, breaking projects down into small steps, using lists to both order and chart progress.
- *Practice* your plan One Day At A Time.

Clearing The Clutter _____

It's been more than 2,000 years since Socrates sauntered through the busy Greek marketplace and considered himself fortunate to need so little of what he saw. How many of the items we have do we actually need?

Is your office, workshop or desk cluttered with unused furniture, obsolete equipment, age-old files or reference materials you haven't consulted in years? Is your home filled with dust-catchers, pictures you no longer see, a lamp you can't stand and sad reminders of times you'd rather forget? Is there so much "stuff" everywhere that just looking at it makes you feel confused?

If you can "clean house" mentally, emotionally and spiritually, you can clear the clutter from your life. This involves getting rid of what you don't use, need, want or enjoy — and rearranging what you do use, need, want or enjoy — so those things work to your comfort and convenience. It's the physical manifestations of Keep It Simple.

Peggy Jones and Pam Young, who wrote *The Sidetracked Home Executives,* perfected this system.

Where to start? At the beginning. Simply take pen and pad in hand and start at an entry point to your home or workplace (or with the room that bugs you the most). Note anything you'd like to change, every item to which you have a negative reaction. Write down how you'd like the room to be.

At home your list might read: "Cracked hallway mirror — throw away. Living room walls — repaint in brighter color. Easy chair I always drank in — re-upholster. Bookcase — thin out. Knickknack shelf — sell salt n' pepper collection, repaint shelf for kids' room. Go for lighter feel in living room with colors I enjoy more." You get the idea?

At work the list might note: "Reception area shabby — repaint and buy green plants. Work tables too close together — move back. Photos remind of sick old days — put up new ones. Desk drawer cluttered — clean out, add deskside filing cabinet. Try for a modern look and more efficient working space."

If it's just your own desk or private workspace you're uncluttering, your list might read: "Calendar — hang a larger one; desktop — remove everything, wash off top and put back only one personal item and file holder; bottom drawer — reorganize and pitch old files. Make area feel clutter-free and pleasant."

Of course you'll want to work with others who may be affected by these changes, considering their needs as well. The point is that you needn't live or work with surroundings that don't foster a sense of serenity. You may not be able to make all the changes immediately but you will have a vision of what you want and a plan of action . . . with plenty of projects to keep you busy for weeks.

Notes To Myself

Notes To Myself

No-Sweat Sorting

Reluctant to discard something you might need someday? Use this gauge: *If you haven't used it, worn it, eaten it, read it or finished it in the last year — pitch it.* If the concept is too shocking, simply pack the item away for six months. If you haven't missed it in that time, you don't need it. Shakespeare noted that "Parting is such sweet sorrow," but it can also bring sweet relief.

A mess-free method of sorting out anything, from drawer to closet, is to take three boxes or bags and label them: Throw Away, Give Away and Put Away.

Dispose of them this way: Throw Away goes out to the trash. Give Away goes into the car trunk for dropping off at a charity collection box. Put Away goes where it is used or stored.

Confine the mess by tackling only one drawer, shelf, closet, room or project at a time. There's no point in making one place look worse in order to get another looking better. Remove the mess, don't just move it.

Consider an annual garage or yard sale — perhaps with neighbors or recovering friends — in spring or late summer to motivate the thinning process. Simply stick labels with prices on each item (a different color label for each seller) and log each sale in a notebook for divvying up later.

How about a swap party? Stack your unwanted things in a corner or on the patio and invite friends to make trades. Or offer unneeded items to someone who could use them. Inquire at recovery half-way houses in your area (such donations are usually tax deductible). The vestiges of our old lives could become welcome additions to another recovering person's new life.

Putting Paper In Its Place

The secret to keeping papers — mail, newspapers, magazines, memos, messages, personal mementos, bills — from inundating your life like a ticker-tape parade is to handle each piece of paper only once.

Notes To Myself

Again, three P's apply to paper:

- *Pitch* it (throw it away).
- *Process* it (pay it, read it, answer it, pass it on, file for later action).
- *Put* it away (file it, put it on a bulletin board or in a scrapbook — put it where it will be kept).

Handling paper only once (or as few times as possible) is best accomplished by . . .

- Taking the paper to the place where you process it (opening mail in your home office area).
- Setting specific times aside for handling types of paperwork (the first or last hour of the day at work to handle correspondence, the last day of the month to pay bills at home).
- Creating a *To File* folder.
- Establishing a filing system.
- Learning what's important and what's not (paper packrats, beware of things that "might come in handy" — grit your teeth and pitch them).
- Regarding your wastebasket as a hungry friend, waiting to be fed (and relieving you of that time-waster, indecision).

We'll look at filing systems in the next section, but let's take a closer look at handling the most pernicious paper problems:

Mail —

To eliminate pieces of mail strung all over the house, sit in one place to open it — preferably in your home office area. Take three or four file folders, boxes or baskets and label them: Pay, Answer and Keep. Weekly and monthly, clean them out, paying bills as they fall due (jotting the due-date on the envelope will remind you), answering correspondence and discarding it and filing away the item you wish to keep.

Work Papers —

Desk tops stay tidier and work becomes easier to perform by using a shelf or divider system. Silcox recommends the labels:

1. *In* (all incoming material, including mail).
2. *To do* (everything you must act on).

Notes To Myself

3. *Out* (all material you've acted upon, including answered mail and memos, to-be-filed, completed reports and budgets. A clerk may collect for distribution or you may do it yourself at the end of the day).
4. *Read* (professional journals, articles, long memos, reports — grab from here to read in spare moments or at lunch, while traveling or waiting).
5. *Meetings* (things prepared for meetings — use a different color of folder for each meeting or organization).

Newspapers, Magazines, Professional Journals

Don't let them stack up. Keep only the articles you need from them.

- Immediately clip items you want to keep for future reference and drop them into a To File folder.
- Rip out long pieces you don't have time to read now and tuck them into your personal notebook for reading in a spare moment.
- Toss newspapers daily (or bundle into discarded grocery bags for recycling).

- Keep unread magazines in one pile. Drop the subscription if you find two or more issues of one publication stacked without your getting to them (if a particular issue catches your eye, buy it at a newsstand).
- Save space by tearing out only articles you want to keep but if you must save entire issues, store them in plastic or cardboard magazine files which can be labeled and stacked on bookshelves.

Messages

Have a central place for all phone and personal messages at home and work. They may be placed under the phone, taped to a mirror, tacked on a bulletin board, written on a chalkboard or held to the refrigerator door with a magnet, but the place should be one used and checked regularly by every member of the household or work department.

Personal Mementos

In addition to a central bulletin board which serves as a household or office message center, personal bulletin boards are handy in children's bedrooms to display artwork, school papers, invitations, activity schedules, recent photographs and other keepsakes. Clean off each bulletin board regularly every month or two, dropping must-save items into a file folder marked with that child's name. Some parents keep individual scrapbooks — a perfect way to organize and preserve school pictures and report cards. New scrapbooks make inexpensive but meaningful Christmas or birthday gifts.

Filing To Find It

Now that we've put paper in its place, how do we keep track of the paper we need to save? The answer is files — not piles.

The To File folder mentioned in the previous section is only a temporary holder for papers you want or need to keep. That one folder at home or at work would grow fat and unwieldy if we didn't empty it weekly into a comprehensive filing system.

That system can range from a few file folders in a kitchen drawer or cardboard carton in a closet to a four-drawer metal filing cabinet. What's important is having a system that enables you to put your hands on what you want when you want it — whether it's a warranty for the lawnmower, last year's cancelled checks or a recovery pamphlet you read last year and kept to pass on.

A filing system can get as detailed as you want, but the key is to Keep It Simple by making broad categories. When in doubt, ask yourself, "What's this about?" Then drop it into the most appropriate file.

A simple portable and absolutely free method for keeping important papers together and getting bills paid on time is to use an old shoebox, with pieces of construction paper folded to hold papers with rubber bands. Label the folders Bank Statements, Bills To Pay, Recovery, Correspondence, Insurance, Receipts, Income Tax Records, Medical.

Notes To Myself

Or buy an inexpensive, cardboard accordian file. Use the headings provided or make up your own. A regular metal file cabinet gives you space for more categories.

Your filing system will reflect your needs and interests. File papers connected with each other will be in the same file. Be careful of the trap of the Miscellaneous file — I avoid one because it's too easy to cram everything there. The same filing principles apply to both home and work files, although work files are more likely to be specific.

Figure out the filing system that works best for you, stick with it and amend it as needed. No one will flunk you in filing. Keep your system as simple or as complex as you like, but do consider some kind of filing plan.

Becoming organized is not impossible. The fact you chose this book demonstrates your determination to end the frustration and confusion of a disordered life.

Remember: Don't agonize — organize!

Notebooks And Lists

Paper remembers so you may forget.

— Anonymous

. . . .

Don't you wish you had a dollar for every scrap of paper on which you've jotted a phone number or a reminder of things to buy — and then lost it before you used it? I could afford a trip around the world by now if I could only find the note with the travel agent's number.

Or how about a buck for each item you tucked away in your head to remember and promptly forgot?

This chapter covers the use of notebooks and lists to unclutter our heads and organize our lives.

Notebooks

The beauty of a notebook reminder system is that there's a definite place to list each thing, and the notebook is always with you. My notebook was the most important tool in my becoming a recovering slob.

Your notebook might hold a variety of categories from phone numbers to shopping lists to work notes to a personal inventory. You may want to tuck in letters to write when you have time, newspaper clippings and a favorite inspirational pamphlet for those moments when you need a quick shot of serenity.

After you've read through this chapter, you might browse through a stationery store or dimestore to help you decide size, expense, headings and amount of information you want to carry with you.

Supplies

The simplest notebook is a pocket-size spiral note pad. It doesn't allow pages to be added but does provide a consistent place in which to jot notes to yourself.

A loose-leaf notebook can grow in sophistication to any size, depending on how organized you want to be and how much weight you want to pack around. Do you want to carry it in

Notes To Myself

Notes To Myself

a breast pocket, brief case, purse or backpack? Some fanatics lug an 8"x10" notebook complete with family photos, but I Keep It Simple with a little 4½"x6½" notebook.

The cost can be as little as 49 cents for the spiral notepad, $10 if you put your loose-leaf notebook together yourself from the dimestore or up to $100 if you buy it ready-made from a stationery or business supply store (and then you'll need refills, which may not always be readily available). Mine is a cheap, dimestore special — notebook, lined paper to fit, dividers with tabs. (You can make your own with index cards and tabs.)

Keep extra sheets in the front for easy jotting; file later under the proper heading. Remember, your notebook needn't weigh a ton. It's merely a temporary place for jotting notes which you'll later discard or file at home or work. On the inside cover, tape your business card or ink in your name and number with PLEASE RETURN noted. Tape a small calendar to the other inside cover or to a divider card.

To get started in the habit of using a personal organizational notebook, you may want to make a daily or weekly To Do list on the very first page. As you refer to it and cross off your accomplishments, the notebook will become a friend. Sunday evenings are a good time to spend a few minutes organizing the next week in your notebook.

Suggested Headings

My own small notebook carries eight basic headings:

Home — weekly To Do list, short-term and long-range projects, household needs.

Work — weekly To Do list, deadlines, notes.

Me — Serenity Prayer, thoughts, meditations, inspirational quotes, books I want to read, etc.

Family, Friends — phone numbers, birthdays.

Notes To Myself

Dates — small calendar, appointments, upcoming events.

Shopping, Money — grocery list, store sales, list of business expenses as I incur them, list of monthly payments I must make.

Writing — notes, brilliant ideas, future projects, memorable quotes.

Floater — special projects as needed (Christmas, Mother's funeral).

Some of these extra headings may suit you:

To Do — at home, work, church, support groups, with headings of Today, This Week, By Deadline.

Books, Letters — books loaned and borrowed, letters owed and sent, addresses.

Recovery — meeting schedule, support group members' phone numbers, birthdays, inventory, relapse warning signs, Serenity Prayer.

Spouse — sizes, needs, wishes, social security number, business schedules, account numbers.

Kids — sizes, needs, activity schedules, friends' numbers.

Appointments — calendar, doctor and dentist numbers, lunch and dinner dates, business meetings.

Addresses, Phone Numbers — family, friends, support group members, doctor and dentist, frequently used numbers.

Inspirational — notes from meetings and/or church, quotes from books and magazines, inspiring thoughts.

Car — repair shop numbers, maintenance dates, registration numbers, insurance numbers, key code.

Hobby — supplies needed, projects to do, club meeting schedules, other hobbyists' phone numbers.

Service Work — meetings, phone numbers, projects.

Birthday Gifts — family and friends' birthday dates (check monthly and add To Do list), ideas, list of what's in home gift box.

To Get — grocery list, things needed for home or work, reminders for dry-cleaning and library books.

Want, Need — lists for each family member.

Notes To Myself

Notes To Myself

Information — credit card numbers, bag size for the vacuum, blood types, insurance policy numbers, etc.

Business — expenses, mileage, projects, reminders.

Medical — phone numbers, dental exams due, kids' shots, allergy notes.

Relationship — mutual goals, activities you might both enjoy, insights on the relationship, a reminder: *Would I rather be right or would I rather be loved?*

Lists — books to read, recommended movies and restaurants, things borrowed and lent, don't-miss events, wishes.

But let's not get compulsive! This notebook is only a tool to help you get organized. There is no right or wrong way. Select the size and system that works best for you. Revamp it and try it at least a month before you give up on it.

Lists

Why make lists? They not only help you remember things, but crossing off an item is proof you're making progress.

If lists intimidate you, consider writing down one thing to do each day — then strike it off with relish. The next day, list two items, gradually working your way up.

The important thing to remember is that lists are merely guides. You can't flunk lists. If you don't get to something, merely carry it over to the next day or week. Don't set unrealistic assignments.

To Do List

I keep two To Do lists — one for the week with headings of home, work and other in my notebook, and one for the day on my desk at work. I make up the weekly list each Sunday evening and add to it as I think of things. The daily work list I make up before leaving work and add to it the following morning and through the day as new tasks arise.

You may prefer getting your lists in order on Sundays or during a quiet breakfast, while commuting on the train or bus or upon sitting down at

Notes To Myself

your desk. The most important thing is jotting down items as they occur to you. Depending on memory alone has helped keep us disorganized all these years.

Feel free to inject a little humor here. Therapist/author Ann Smith suggests making a list of things you have no intention of ever doing. Then don't do them! This is especially good for perfectionists.

At the bottom of your daily or weekly To Do list, add a little reward for yourself.

Grocery Lists

The most frequently made lists must be for groceries, so let's begin there. It's too easy to forget what's needed and to buy on impulse, running your grocery bill even higher. I jot down items as I notice they are needed, adding to the list before heading for the grocery store.

Some organizational wizards type and copy a master list: staples, canned food, beverages, spices, frozen food, meats, produce, paper, personal items, cleaning, pets, etc. They check the item as supplies run low then restock, so they never actually run out. Simply having a Shopping section in my notebook to jot down needed supplies works fine for me.

Types Of Lists

The types of lists you'll want to keep depend on your family responsibilities, degree of involvement in service or volunteer work and degree of organization you want.

You may want to use lists for birthdays and anniversaries (including sobriety birthdays), bills due, books you want to read or have lent out, goals (personal and professional), letters owed, things needed for the house, clothing needed, personal inventory, gifts you plan to buy, support group members' phone numbers, homework assignments, rewards for incentives, etc.

These are suggestions for you to choose from. There are no musts,

Notes To Myself

Notes To Myself

shoulds and ought-tos here. Recovery is about seeing our choices. So is organization.

SIX

You

If we do not change our direction, we are likely to end up where we are headed.

— Chinese Proverb

. . . .

You may wonder, "How can I take time for myself or think just of myself when I so selfishly robbed my family and job of time when I was practicing my disease? I owe them all the time I can give."

If you're feeling this way, it shows you're conscientious and trying to do the right thing — in short, trying hard to work your program. But let's not get compulsive or drown in guilt.

We can give to others only when we have something, someone (ourselves) to give. As we've learned, practicing an addiction leaves little of ourselves and precious little time for sharing what we have left. When we fail to regain and maintain a sense of self, we feel depleted again.

To make one's sense of contentment a priority is not selfish, it's self-full. Only when you are full, can you give generously.

If you feel guilty about taking time for yourself, it's acknowledging that you feel you don't really deserve it. And that's an element of co-dependence.

Time For Yourself

We need time alone to recharge our batteries, focus on our desires, take our inventory, meditate and collect our thoughts. If you find yourself thinking or saying, "I wish I had the time to . . ." or "If I only had the time, once a week I'd . . ." — then arrange for that time now and do it.

Don't ask permission for taking time for yourself. Don't apologize for doing it — simply announce your plans. Some practiced caretakers have more trouble with this. We tend to make sure everyone else is taken care of before we take care of ourselves. We must remember that we are not only fostering our own growth, we are helping others grow by inferring they are capable of caring for them-

Notes To Myself

Notes To Myself

selves. Thoughtful leave-taking is not abandonment.

Let's face it — we make time for things we truly want to do. So we have to want to make time for ourselves. It may help to start on a small scale with five minutes of relaxation, a half-hour in a hot bath. Work your way up to an afternoon off, an evening out, a Saturday to yourself, an occasional weekend away. I'll never forget the Mother's Day I spent doing only what I wanted — which included brunch with my children, Renee, Michelle and Keith. But I didn't once say yes when I meant no. The entire day was delicious.

Pack a few "me days" into your week. Consider it as nurturing your soul, filling your tank, stoking your fire.

A Place For Yourself

Part of regaining a sense of self is having a place to call your own. Ideally, this is a room — a place decorated in your own taste and the space to leave out projects no one else is allowed to touch. Is there a spare bedroom or part of the basement, attic or even the garage you could make your own?

If not, settle for a nook. This might be a corner of the den, kitchen, livingroom, bedroom or even a spare closet you could outfit as your own private place to work, do hobbies, write letters, meditate, keep your recovery literature, make phone calls and read.

No room for a nook? Then settle for a special place, even if it's just a chair or corner of the couch. Announce it as your own. Put your special touch on it with a pillow you like, a favorite picture or a copy of the Serenity Prayer, a place for your coffee cup, books and a good reading light. A wooden lap desk kept next to the chair can hold stationery supplies or a magazine rack can hold your favorite magazines.

Travel, Vacations

Whether you're traveling on business or pleasure, some pre-planning and organization will remove much of the fuss and add to the fun.

Before you go . . .

- Buy maps and guidebooks (they're cheapest at used book stores) and enjoy planning your trip ahead of time. It makes you a more appreciative traveller and it can save you money.
- Buy traveller's checks; remember to carry the receipt in a different place from your checks.
- If traveling to a foreign country, obtain some of that currency from the international department of a large bank. You can familiarize yourself with the bills and exchange value, thus feeling more comfortable when you arrive. Plus you don't have to exchange money right away.
- Arrange with a neighbor or friend to collect your mail and newspapers so they don't stack up to signal to burglars that you're gone. Don't forget to arrange for care of plants and pets.

Perhaps you can work out a trade with someone. You return the favor when they vacation.

- Leave your itinerary — route, flight numbers, hotels, license plate, etc., with a co-worker, babysitter or friend in case of emergency.
- Invest in a suitcase with built-in wheels — or add a shoulder strap to better distribute the weight. Or carry only a backpack. (I've spent two months touring Mexico and three weeks doing Europe with only a small pack.) A backpack makes you more mobile. You simply wash clothes out more often.

Some suggestions for packing:

- Keep It Simple is the theme. If you can't wear an item with two or three coordinates, don't bring it. After you pack, remove half of the stuff.
- Men and women can both ask double-duty of the clothes they take — a big shirt or cover-up can serve as beach and pool jacket, bathrobe and nightshirt. A pair of sandals can be used as slippers, beach or pool wear plus wearing out to dinner.

Notes To Myself

- If there's some article of clothing you're lacking, fine. Shop for it at your destination. It's fun to sport local wear and it makes a worthwhile souvenir.
- Stock your toilet kit with small, inexpensive samples from the drug or dimestore. Find aftershave, shampoo, conditioner, toothpaste, deodorant, liquid soap, bubble bath, hand lotion, mouth wash, suntan oil, bandages, antacids.
- Carry scented, pre-moistened towelettes for quick freshen-ups and hand-washing.
- Pack a nylon duffle bag, folded in your suitcase, to hold the extra clothes and souvenirs you'll acquire. Check it through when full.
- Bring a light backpack. Use it as your allowable carry-on aboard the plane to hold reading material and perhaps a sweater for in-flight (and perhaps a change of underwear and toilet articles in case luggage is delayed). Then use it for camera, guidebook, beach towel, sunglasses, sweater, map. Stow lunch, souvenirs, snacks.

It leaves your hands free, is harder to steal than a purse and readies you for a variety of activities without having to go back to the hotel room.

- Bring a heating coil (and adapter for foreign travel) and packets (or sealable plastic bags) of coffee, tea, hot chocolate, soup, creamer and sugar for in-room pick-me-ups. Buy some fruit and sweet rolls for breakfast in your room at one-third the price of a restaurant meal.
- Unpack promptly, hanging garments on a hanger in the bathroom to steam out wrinkles while you shower.

On your way:

- If flying makes you nervous, distract yourself. Do paperwork, write postcards, read an engrossing novel, watch the movie, listen to music, read recovery material, meditate.

  Now's a good time for the Serenity Prayer. If the flight gets bumpy, imagine the plane suspended on a rubber band, wrapped around God's finger. If ever there was a perfect time to practice Letting Go and Letting God, this is it.

• Try a support group meeting wherever you are — even in a foreign language, the spirit is there. It reinforces the notion you have friends wherever you go. And the variety of people is fascinating. Check for time and places through the Yellow Pages, Traveller's Aid office or U.S. Consul's office. Hold your own meeting. Make an announcement or post a notice inviting friends of Bill W., adult children, etc. This backfired once at a broadcasting convention where a Bill Wilson was registered. His buddies showed up, ready to party!

Finances a problem? Consider . . .

• Going camping. Enjoy nature's solitude alone or invite recovering friends to join you.
• Can't get away for two or three weeks? Take a day here and two days there to enjoy a long weekend relaxing at home, driving around the state, making a fellowship convention in another town.
• Off to a business convention? Taking a week's vacation afterward near the

convention site will drastically cut your travel expenses if your company is paying for the round trip.

- If you can't afford to go away at all, stage a retreat at home. Notify friends and family that you'll be unavailable for a time, then unplug your phone. Sleep, watch old movies, stay in your jammies all day, read all night, write in your journal, stare out the window at the birds. I did this for four days one December when I'd become exhausted from compulsively doing too much. It was the perfect gift to myself.

Heading Off Crisis

It's often life's little frustrations that can tip us toward relapse. There is plenty of helpful material on relapse prevention. This section is about warding off difficulties before they become a mini-crisis. You've handled biggies — don't let the little things throw you.

Plan ahead. Consider . . .

- Keeping change for last-minute bus fares, laundry, lunches and field trips in

__Notes To Myself__

a designated "kitty." Ask for a roll of quarters when you bank to keep the kitty stocked.

- Keeping change in the car for parking meters and tolls.
- Making sure children carry "emergency" information with them — along with parental permission for emergency medical treatment (always leave with sitters).
- Arranging with a neighbor, co-worker or recovering friend for on-call emergency rides, child-watching, support group aid or child pick-up.
- Leaving enough unused credit on charge cards to afford emergency car repair, air fare.
- Keeping a spare house key in your car, wallet or with a neighbor. Keeping a spare car key in the house, wallet or magnetized holder under the bumper.
- Keeping financial accounts in both spouse's names or an adult child's or trusted friend's or lawyer's so the other person can get at savings or checking if you are suddenly incapacitated.

Filling the gas tank as soon as it hits the quarter-full mark.

- Making sure your address is clearly visible to emergency vehicles.
- Learning cardiopulmonary resuscitation (CPR). Check with your local fire department or hospital for classes. Just months after completing a course offered through my company, I had occasion to give CPR to a man who suffered a heart attack next to me in a restaurant. I don't know whether he lived or died, but it felt so good to feel helpful instead of helpless.
- Having a brief list of clothes to take for an emergency trip, along with a packed toilet kit.

Wardrobe

Ignore this section if you have an outfit for every day of the year, a nursemaid dresses the kids or your clothes are laid out each morning by your valet.

The rest of us will save time, money and agonizing indecision by coor-

Notes To Myself

dinating our wardrobe. It works for men, women and children. You simply pick three coordinating colors (or several shades of the same color) and buy suits and separates in those colors. No matter how color-blind, sound asleep or fashion-oblivious you are, you'll always look together.

For example, women or kids could choose red, white and blue. You could grab a blue skirt, red shirt and white jacket — or any other combination — and look great. The kids can dress themselves with no problem and still look presentable.

Men might select brown, beige and light blue. In brown pants, beige jacket, light blue shirt and tie of brown and blue, you'll look sharp anywhere.

To Keep It Really Simple, stick to one color in various shades. This is a good way to keep children's clothes organized, especially if you have several kids.

Wardrobes can be updated by adding trendy accessories — a bolo tie or big sweater. When shopping for accessories, wear the outfit, rather than depending on your memory to match colors.

As a reward to yourself, you may want to indulge in a color analysis (for both men and women) to determine which colors look best on you. The color counselor will give you color swatches to make wardrobe coordination even easier.

SPECIAL PROJECTS

Wondering what to do with the free time and energy recovery brings? Here's a suggestion for each week of the year:

1. Make a will.
2. Clean a closet.
3. Look for a new job.
4. Redecorate.
5. Go back to school.
6. Organize a garage sale.
7. Update a photo album.
8. Set up a filing system.
9. Plan a vacation.
10. Catch up on correspondence.
11. Put recipes in order.
12. Start a support group closer to home.

Notes To Myself

Notes To Myself

13. Shop for a new car or clean and organize your old one.
14. Plan for Christmas.
15. Organize your work place.
16. Do your spring cleaning (no matter what time of year).
17. Hold a family reunion.
18. Give a party.
19. Start a hobby.
20. Buy property.
21. Organize books, records, tapes.
22. Refinish furniture.
23. Train the dog.
24. Learn to cook.
25. Take a CPR course.
26. Master driving.
27. Remodel the house.
28. Learn to swim.
29. Landscape the yard.
30. Take a self-improvement course.
31. Make a budget.
32. Organize the kitchen.
33. Move.
34. Read a novel or a self-help book.
35. Thin out the clutter, room by room.
36. Buy a computer.
37. Go for marriage counseling.
38. Learn a foreign language.

39. Become a sponsor in your recovery group.
40. Lose weight.
41. Muck out the basement or attic.
42. Assess your relationships.
43. Sign up for a parenting course.
44. Begin an exercise program.
45. Take up a sport.
46. Develop spiritually: read inspirational material, go to church or shop for one.
47. Make new friends.
48. Volunteer.
49. Research your family's genealogy.
50. Improve your relationship with your parents/children.
51. Take a night class.
52. Go on a private weekend retreat.

Add some of your own ideas:

_____

_____

_____

_____

Rewarding Yourself _____

Recovery and organization are rewards in themselves, rewards we

Notes To Myself

Notes To Myself

appreciate more fully each day. Yet both take effort. Recognize that effort, that conscientiousness, by setting aside an hour a day for yourself, doing anything you want. It will add to your serenity.

Maybe when we're 80 years old, abstinent for 50 years and genuinely mature, we won't need rewards. Until then, let's offer ourselves some other incentives. Being good to ourselves is a part of successful recovery.

You may want to make two lists, "smallies" for accomplishing daily tasks you would rather have ignored and "biggies" for getting everything finished on your weekly To Do list.

It might look something like this:

SMALLIES
Watching a favorite TV show
Seeing a movie
Taking a coffee break
Relaxing for a half-hour
Working on a hobby
Lunching with a friend
Taking a walk

BIGGIES

Signing up for a class
Dining out
Planning a dream vacation
Taking a whole day for me
Buying a bicycle
Getting a massage
Buying a teddy bear

Add some ideas of your own:

- _____
- _____
- _____
- _____
- _____
- _____
- _____
- _____

In summarizing this chapter, let's remember that if we put ourselves last, we are often put last by others.

If you feel you must justify time for yourself because of all the time you took driving, gambling, using, binge-eating, remember that time was used escaping yourself.

Now it is time to find yourself. You can give to others only in proportion

Notes To Myself

to what you have to give. An empty bucket can quench no one's thirst. In recovery, we fill our buckets.

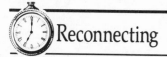

SEVEN

Reconnecting

No man is an island.

— John Donne

. . . .

Addictions and co-dependence are lonely. We may have surrounded ourselves with other people in order to look "normal," but deep inside we knew we needed our substance or our compulsive behavior more than we needed anyone.

In recovery we rediscover not only ourselves but others. Looking out through clear eyes we can appreciate people for the fascinating individuals they are — without judging them, without sizing up just what they can do for us. Our self-induced isolation has ended, but it takes time to build our self-confidence, to reach out without feeling awkward.

Never before have we had so much to give to loved ones and strangers alike. When we doubt ourselves or our social skills, let us remember that. We no longer need to substitute money, expensive gifts or false promises for the most valuable thing we have to share: Us. Recovery has wrapped us in a big red ribbon.

Yet reconnecting — like recovery — is a process. It takes daily practice, even work. But the rewards are sweet.

That Special Person

Addiction takes its toll on relationships, we all know that, but even recovery can be threatening as people and their patterns of living change.

We can help heal old wounds with a long-time partner — or avoid the old pitfalls with a new one — by . . .

- Making our spouse or special person a part of our recovery by inviting them to an open support group meeting, encouraging them to attend one of their own, reading literature, enrolling in family counseling.
- Introducing them to our recovering friends and helping them feel part of things, rather than left out.
- Planning specific time together . . . evenings alone, nights out, weekday lunches, weekend brunches, weekends without children, long walks, picnics.

- Playing together, laughing together. How long has it been since you've had a water or pillow fight?
- Working on a project together. Can you both remodel the basement, enroll in a language class?
- Planning toward a common goal. Where do you want to be a couple five years from now? Is this the time to talk about the cross-country trip you've only dreamed about?
- Making time for lovemaking. Go to bed early, send the children to a sitter's, go to a motel for the night.

Singles, take heart. There are places and ways to meet other people outside bars. Consider . . .

- Fellowship activities and conventions.
- Service work.
- Community volunteer work.
- Night classes.
- Singles and single parents' groups.
- Couples and relatives — they all know single people.

Instead of searching for Mr. or Ms. Right, consider *becoming* it. Self-

esteem and social confidence grow as
we reach out to others in recovery.

Children

Children may be the ones our disease hurt most. Yet they may be the
most easily forgiving, so great is their
need for our love and approval, no
matter what their age.

And they certainly can be a great
source of joy in our new-found recovery, whether they live with us,
with the other parent or are grown
and on their own.

Perhaps the greatest gifts we can
offer our children are . . .

Time — Children may clamor for
things, but what they long for deep-
down is our time and attention. It's
easy to fall into the trap (especially
for divorced weekend parents) of
thinking we must constantly entertain
our children. Instead of dragging
them through the zoo, movie matinee
and pizza parlor, what's wrong with
riding bikes, taking walks, playing a
game or sharing a TV program over a
bowl of popcorn?

Notes To Myself

Notes To Myself

Even sharing chores provides time together. "Quality time" has become a buzzword as "quantity" seems to diminish — oddly enough, in the name of "saving time."

I recall extolling the long-anticipated joy of a dishwasher to a friend, who retorted, "And what do you plan to do with all the time you save?" Good question. Looking back over the years, I recall many good conversations over shared chores of washing and drying dishes, but not one over a humming dishwasher.

Chore-sharing and driving together provide opportunities for casual conversation — especially with teenagers, who frequently clam up at the parental inquisition: "How is school? Who are you going out with tonight? What are you thinking about?" Some extended time together provides the opportunity for conversation to occur naturally and the child to open up in a relaxed atmosphere.

Some parents choose to have regular "dates" with a child, which may include going to dinner and a movie, a hamburger and play in the park — whatever appeals to both parent and child, and suits the child's age level and the parent's pocketbook. This is a good way for a parent with several children to offer special undivided attention.

Making an extra effort to attend a sporting event, school program or scouting or club activity in which the child participates also is a gift of one's time. Just knowing a parent is watching and rooting among the spectators makes a child feel loved.

Keep Promises — Ask a child of an actively addicted parent what hurts most and "broken promises" is invariably near the top of the list. Keeping our promises is a way of making amends, healing old wounds and ensuring a happier relationship with our children.

The best way to keep a promise is not to make them casually. Children take things very literally, even our speculative "Maybe we'll go fishing next weekend" may feel like a promise

Notes To Myself

to them. Rather than making general statements, we can mention specific times and/or circumstances. "Let's save next Saturday morning and afternoon to go fishing" or "We'll go fishing the weekend after you bring home a report card which proves you're doing better in math."

It might help both parent and child to write down a promised event on the calendar. If something important occurs and the date can't be kept, try making the promise postponed, rather than broken by explaining the delay to the child and promptly rebooking the engagement.

Keeping promises can help us be on time, plan our time and become better organized. Most importantly, it can demonstrate our good will toward the little people who want so much to believe us.

Availability — This doesn't mean catering to a child's every whim or demand for attention. It simply means providing reassurance that we can be counted on.

We become available to our children by . . .

- Actively listening. This means we put down our newspaper, turn off the television and look at the person talking. We let them talk without giving nonverbal or verbal responses that shut them off (looking bored, putting them down). And we don't start solving their problems or giving advice until it's asked for.
- Spending time alone. As mentioned above, this may include walks or drives, doing chores, scheduled dates, just puttering around the house. It can involve reading to your children or simply tucking in older ones.
- Touching them frequently. Little ones are easy to be affectionate with but older ones resist being treated "like babies." Yet quick hugs, pats on the back or a tousling of hair as the child passes provide assurance that we are there and that we care. Such touching can go far in diffusing strained relations with teenagers — and even our mates.

• Encouraging their healing. Because addiction affects the entire family, everyone needs to begin recovery. Initiating conversation and allowing frank feelings about both the "bad old days" of active addiction and the sometimes confusing adjustments to sobriety and abstinence can help children with this transition. You may wish to supply recovery books written for children and support group literature such as Ala-Tot and Ala-teen. You may choose to involve them in their own support groups, or invite them to yours. The most important thing is being open with your feelings and emphasizing that it's now safe for them to be open about their own feelings.

Gift-Giving

Card-sending and gift-giving are the least of the addicted person's concerns. In recovery they can be a joy — and a thoughtful way of making amends.

One easy way to remedy gift-buying blues is to buy things on sale throughout the year. They may be suitable for anyone or something bought especially with an individual in mind. Some of my best Christmas gifts for next year are snapped up December 26. My bargain gifts go into one big box. I keep gift wrapping paper, bows and tags in another box. When a birthday comes up, I just dig into both boxes and wrap. I reach into my file folder of cards (bought as I find amusing or especially appropriate ones) and bingo, I'm ready for any occasion. This system also saves me money, especially when the holidays roll around.

You may want to keep a greeting card file in your home office (or in your desk at work). Note important dates (don't forget sobriety birthdays) on a calendar. You'll even be covered when a co-worker suddenly announces it's his birthday. Some well-organized people address cards immediately and note the mail date in the corner which will be covered by the stamp.

Notes To Myself

What a way to thrill and amaze your friends by never being late again.

Entertaining, Holidays

Intimidated by the notion of throwing a party — especially without booze and drugs as "entertainment?" It may take a successful shindig to reassure you, but clean and sober partying is the best kind of all. Good spirits don't come out of a bottle. They come from good friends who aren't afraid to be open.

Successful entertaining doesn't have to cost lots of money or depend on gourmet meals in a lavish setting. Which would you rather have — silver dessert forks and shallow dinner conversation or hearty laughter over take-out pizza while sitting on a friend's floor? Remember, most people — especially the understanding new friends you're meeting in recovery — care more about good talk than fancy food or fine furniture.

Take the hassle out of entertaining by . . .

- Having a potluck. Everyone brings a main dish, salad or dessert. You supply the coffee and soft drinks and perhaps some bread.
- Asking guests to pick up take-out food — pizza, ice cream, donuts, Chinese food, hamburgers.
- Having friends over for dessert. Ice cream and coffee can be managed by anyone.
- Drawing a map to your house and making copies as needed.
- Joining other recovering people in a "progressive party." Guests move from home to home for each course.
- Meeting at a park for a picnic.
- Offering to buy coffee for folks after a support group meeting.
- Asking party guests to bring a friend, in order to increase your circle of healthy acquaintances.
- Forgetting the cleaning until afterward. Light a few candles for a romantic glow — no one will see the dust.

Holidays and special anniversaries can be a painful time, especially for recovering people who remain

Notes To Myself

estranged from family and old friends. Instead of feeling sorry for yourself and risking relapse, consider . . .

- Throwing a birthday, sobriety birthday, new job or new house party for yourself.
- Inviting in other people who are alone, newly recovering, new to town — or those who would enjoy a few hours away from a home still insane with addiction.
- Experiencing the delights of small children during the holidays by having in people with kids, offering to take neighbors' children Christmas shopping or babysitting them (and holding a cookie-baking session) while their parents shop.
- Asking friends in for a tree-trimming party.
- Donating time to those who need you . . . visiting hospitals, taking goodies to such holiday-workers as police, firefighters, treatment center counselors, serving meals to the needy. We give thanks for recovery by serving Thanksgiving dinners at

a Salvation Army treatment center on skid row.
- Throwing a sober New Year's bash. Write regrets on slips of paper and reconcile them to the past by pitching them into a fireplace or burning bowl. Write resolutions or simple statements of gratitude on balloons and send them soaring at midnight.

List some activities to celebrate your joy of recovery:

_____
_____
_____

Reconnecting with others involves reaching out. We needn't feel self-conscious, because a sober, clean, abstinent self — with a good measure of humor, enthusiasm, honesty and caring — is the best gift we can offer.

Bibliography

Allred, Tamera Smith. **From Diapers to Deadlines** (Liberty Press; 1982).

Bradshaw, John. **Bradshaw On: The Family** (Health Communications Inc.; 1988).

Lakein, Alan. **How To Get Control Of Your Time And Your Life** (New American Library; 1974).

Oliver-Diaz, Philip and Patricia A. O'Gorman. **12 Steps To Self-Parenting** (Health Communications Inc.; 1988).

Peck, Dr. M. Scott. **The Road Less Traveled** (Simon & Schuster, 1978).

Silcox, Diana. **Woman Time** (Wyden Books; 1980).

Smith, Ann. **Overcoming Perfectionism** (Health Communications Inc.; 1990).

Winston, Stephanie. **Getting Organized** (Warner Books; 1979).

Young, Pam and Peggy Jones. **Sidetracked Home Executives** (Warner Books; 1981).

Changes
MAGAZINE

$18* per year for 6 bimonthly issues!

Every issue of **Changes** brings you valuable information on personal recovery concerns like self-esteem, intimacy, and spirituality.
Subscribe today!

Just return the coupon below, or call toll-free (800) 851-9100.
And give the operator this code: HB212

- -

□ YES!

Please enter my subscription to *Changes* Magazine at the special introductory rate of just $18*.

Name: _____

Address: _____

City: _____

State: _____ Zip: _____

Payment method:

□ Payment enclosed   □ Bill me

□ Charge my   □ VISA   □ MC

Acct. #: _____

Exp. Date: _____ Sig: _____

Mail to: CHANGES MAGAZINE   HB212
         Subscription Services
         3201 S.W. 15th Street
         Deerfield Beach, FL 33442-8190

*Florida residents add 6% sales tax. Canadian orders add $20; foreign orders add $31. Please allow 4-6 weeks for delivery.